CATHOLIC MYSTICISM
&
THE BEAUTIFUL LIFE OF GRACE

SCIENCE
of
SAINTHOOD

SCIENCE of SAINTHOOD

Nihil Obstat
The Reverend James M. Dunfee, MA, STL
Censor Librorum
March 9, 2025

Imprimatur
The Most Reverend Edward M. Lohse, JCD
Apostolic Administrator of Steubenville
March 11, 2025

The *nihil obstat* and *imprimatur* do not signify agreement with the content, opinions, or statements expressed but simply affirm that the content does not contradict faith and morals.

Copyright © 2021 Science of Sainthood. All rights reserved.

Scripture verses are from The Revised Standard Version of the Bible: Catholic Edition, copyright © 1965, 1966 the Division of Christian Education of the National Council of the Churches of Christ in the United States of America. Used by permission. All rights reserved.

Written by Matthew Leonard
Graphic Design by Patty Borgman

Science Of Sainthood | ScienceOfSainthood.com

Table of Contents

Welcome to the Science of Sainthood — 4

Quick Start Guide to Catholic Meditation — 7

Lesson One: What is the Mystical Life? — 11

Lesson Two: The Importance of Station in Life — 15

Lesson Three: How Deification Happens — 19

Lesson Four: The Desire for Divinity — 23

Lesson Five: The Power of Love to Divinize — 27

Lesson Six: The Beauty of Grace — 33

Lesson Seven: Why Do We Struggle? Unpacking the "Absolute Supernatural" — 37

Lesson Eight: Why Do We Struggle? Understanding the "Relative Supernatural" — 41

Lesson Nine: Sanctifying Grace & Our Formal Participation in God — 47

Lesson Ten: The "Accident" of Sanctifying Grace — 51

Lesson Eleven: Understanding the Two Regions of the Human Soul — 55

Lesson Twelve: The Fall from Grace — 59

Lesson Thirteen: Introduction to Actual Grace & Free Will — 65

Lesson Fourteen: Operating Grace vs Cooperating Grace — 69

Welcome to the Science of Sainthood

Welcome to *Catholic Mysticism & the Beautiful Life of Grace*, presented by the Science of Sainthood.

Founded by evangelist Matthew Leonard, the Science of Sainthood is one of the world's premiere online Catholic communities dedicated to teaching authentic Catholic spirituality. Steeped in the tradition of saints like John of the Cross, Teresa of Avila, and Thomas Aquinas, our goal is to guide regular Catholics, step by step, down the path to nothing less than sainthood.

More than education, this is *transformation*!

How To Use This Workbook

Each lesson in this study contains the following sections:

- Short Introduction
- Review of Previous Lesson
- Lesson Video
- Space to Take Notes on the Video Lesson
- A Passage from a Saint
- A Passage from Sacred Scripture for Lectio Divina
- Written Meditation
- Review & Discussion Questions*
- Prayer Journal

How you use the sections depends completely on what works best for you or your group. The written sections are there for either group or individual use. Some groups simply discuss the video and leave the journaling and other content for use outside the group. Other groups work their way through each portion as a whole group, reading the passages aloud. Again, it's entirely up to your discretion.

Given the short duration of the initial videos, We suggest your first meeting consist of watching the "Quick Start Guide to Catholic Meditation" and Lesson One.

The rest of the videos are roughly 10 minutes long. This means it would be quite easy to do two lessons in one group study session. That said, the material is designed for flexibility. Again, use it however it fits your group.

As you can see, we have provided Review and Discussion Questions to help spur group discussion.

Finally, don't forget that this study is just the first of many powerful courses available in the Science of Sainthood.

For information on individual or group enrollment in the Science of Sainthood, visit **ScienceOfSainthood.com**.

With the exception of the Quick Start to Catholic Meditation

In a Group Study But Want to Watch on Your Own, Too?

Enjoy the course on your own time with a great discount on a One Year rental of *Catholic Mysticism & the Beautiful Life of Grace*.

It's the perfect way to get as much as possible out of this study!

Scan the QR Code with your Phone's Camera & Tap the Link!

Quick Start Guide To Catholic Meditation

Lesson Introduction

In order to really dive into the Science of Sainthood and allow the material to transform your life, it's important to begin praying your way through it. In particular, you need to engage in authentic Catholic meditation. While this is something covered in more detail in a later portion of the Science of Sainthood series, we have provided a Quick Start Guide to get you going.

If you would like to read more on the subject of Catholic meditation, check out Matthew Leonard's book *Prayer Works: Getting a Grip on Catholic Spirituality* available at ScienceOfSainthood.com or through retailers.

Regardless, don't skip this vital step. Prayer is the key to the spiritual life!

Notes

What The Saints Say

ST. PETER ALCANTARA was the 16th century confessor for St. Teresa of Avila. The following is an excerpt from *A Treatise on Meditation and Prayer*. (St. Peter attributes the advice to St. Bonaventure.)

"If you would suffer patiently the adversities and miseries of this life, be a man of prayer.

If you would gain power and strength to overcome the temptations of the enemy, be a man of prayer.

If you would mortify your will with all its affections and lusts, be a man of prayer.

If you would understand the cunning devices of Satan, and defend yourself against his deceits, be a man of prayer.

If you would live joyfully, and with sweetness walk in the path of penitence and sorrow, be a man of prayer.

If you would drive out the troublesome gnats of vain thoughts and cares from your soul, be a man of prayer.

If you would sustain your soul with the richness of devotion, and keep it ever full of good thoughts and desires, be a man of prayer.

If you would strengthen and confirm your heart in the pilgrimage with God, be a man of prayer.

Lastly, if you would root out from your soul every vice and in their place plant the virtues, be a man of prayer, for in this is obtained the unction and grace of the Holy Spirit who teaches all things....

And besides all this, if you would climb to the height of contemplation, and delight in the sweet embraces of the Bridegroom, exercise yourself in prayer, for this is the way by which the soul mounts up to contemplation and to the taste of heavenly things."

Lectio Divina

Lectio Divina is Latin for "divine reading." It's basically reading and praying over sacred Scripture and it's easily one of the most powerful forms of meditative prayer.

As we make our way through this study, you will see selections from Scripture that are provided as material for prayer. This first one is taken from Psalm 1. After the Gospels, Psalms is perhaps the most popular book over which to pray.

The Psalms seem to cover the gamut of human emotion and experience. So it's appropriate that our first passage is taken right from the very beginning:

> "Blessed is the man who walks not in the counsel of the wicked, nor stands in the way of sinners, nor sits in the seat of scoffers; but his delight is in the law of the Lord, and on his law he meditates day and night.
>
> He is like a tree planted by streams of water, that yields its fruit in its season, and its leaf does not wither. In all that he does, he prospers.
>
> The wicked are not so, but are like chaff which the wind drives away.
>
> Therefore the wicked will not stand in the judgment, nor sinners in the congregation of the righteous; for the Lord knows the way of the righteous, but the way of the wicked will perish."
>
> PSALM 1

Meditation

What does it mean to meditate on the law of the Lord? At its core, it means developing a deep relationship with God. More specifically, it means entering into regular, interior conversation with the Divine Other who made us.

And this is necessary. Why? Because we need a change in orientation.

As we progress through the Science of Sainthood, one of the main ideas that will take "center stage" is that much of our spiritual ascent depends on shifting our gaze away from ourselves and toward God.

Prayer helps us turn our gaze outward and upward. It helps us to **see** God more clearly and hear what he is asking of us. It also gives us the grace to respond. In other words, prayer is not simply a passive exercise.

We meditate so as to change. We meditate to become like Jesus Christ.

Prayer Journal

LESSON ONE

What is the Mystical Life?

Lesson Introduction

It's important to define the mystical life up front. Not all of us are called to be mystics, but we're all called to the mystical life.

Notes

What The Saints Say

"However quietly we speak, He is so near that He will hear us: we need no wings to go in search of Him but have only to find a place where we can be alone and look upon Him present within us."

ST. TERESA OF AVILA – *16th Century Spanish Mystic & Doctor of the Church*

Lectio Divina

"I came to cast fire upon the earth; and would that it were already kindled!"

LUKE 12:49

Meditation

It's common for people to read this verse in Luke 12 and associate it solely with anger, judgment, and destruction. And certainly there are instances in Scripture where this is the case.

Sodom and Gomorrah were destroyed by fire in Genesis 19. The sons of Aaron were devoured by flames when they offered unholy sacrifice in Leviticus 10. Christ even describes fire as the means by which the city which rejected the king's wedding feast was destroyed in Matthew 22.

So there's certainly a negative connotation with fire. But Christ is talking about something different.

He's talking about setting the *world* on fire with the Holy Spirit.

"This fire is that of the Holy Ghost who must animate, inflame, purify, and perfect us, transforming us to the point of deification," says the great Spanish Dominican Fr. John Arintero. *Arintero, John G. O.P. (1978)* The Mystical Evolution Volume *(p. 23).* Rockford: Tan Books

And as John the Baptist declared in John 3:15, "I baptize you with water; but he who is mightier than I is coming, the thong of whose sandals I am not worthy to untie; he will baptize you with the Holy Spirit and with fire."

Review Questions

1. What is the goal of the mystical life?

2. If we're not all called to be "mystics," is there an "ordinary path" to holiness? What is it traditionally called? What does it include?

3. Why is it difficult even for true mystics like John of the Cross and Teresa of Avila to describe the mystical life?

Discussion Questions

1. Why do you think every single person ever created is called to the mystical life? Is it truly possible for everyone to be a saint?

2. Are there things you can already identify in your life that would keep you from the mystical life?

Prayer Journal

LESSON TWO

The Importance of Station in Life

What We Covered in Our Last Lesson

The mystical life is the hidden life. It is the interior process of becoming more and more like Christ, of being transformed by Him. It's a process of formation and growth through which we become what we were made to be from the very beginning - the image and likeness of Jesus Christ. While Adam and Eve were made in both that image and likeness (though not completely), there's a sense in which humanity lost its likeness to God when sin entered the picture. The whole Catholic life is all about trying to re-acquire that lost likeness and fully joining the Divine Family. That is the underlying goal of the mystical life.

Though not all are going to be "mystics," so to speak, every single one of us is called to the mystical life. That said, most of us take the more traditional route through what is called "asceticism," the name of the ordinary path, or "stages" of Christian perfection. This "ordinary path" includes the basics of the "science of sainthood" like learning how to meditate well, how to grow in virtue, and root out the vice that strangles our spiritual life.

In its highest form, mysticism is the prelude to glory, or foretaste of future happiness, says St. Thomas Aquinas. It's where the soul seems to actually taste, touch, and feel the things of faith, instead of just seeing them from afar.

Lesson Introduction

While the pursuit of perfection is just as valid for us as it is for the guy in a cave reading Latin from the light of a beeswax candle, our path will look a bit different... thankfully.

In his classic work *Introduction to the Devout Life*, St. Francis de Sales makes a very important point with regard to devotion. Namely, that our devotion has to correspond to our station in life.

Notes

What The Saints Say

"In the creation God commanded the plants to bring forth their fruits, each one according to its kind; even so He commands all Christians, who are living plants of the Church, to bring forth their fruits of devotion, each one according to his quality and vocation.

Devotion ought to be differently exercised by the prince, by the gentleman, by the tradesman, by the servant, by the widow, by the maid, and by the married person: and not only so, but the practice also of devotion must be accommodated to the health, the capacity, the employment, and the obligations of each one in particular.

For, I pray thee, would it be fit for a bishop to be as retired as a Carthusian; and if the married people should store up no more than Capuchins, if the tradesman should be all day in the church like a monk, and the religious continually exposed to all exterior exercises of charity for the service of his neighbour as the bishop, would not this devotion be ridiculous, preposterous, and insupportable?

This fault, nevertheless, happens very often, and the world, which does not, or will not discern any difference between real devotion and the indiscretion of those who pretend to be devout, blames and murmurs at it, which cannot remedy such disorders."

ST. FRANCIS DE SALES – *17th Century French Bishop of Geneva & Celebrated Spiritual Writer*

Lectio Divina

"For the body does not consist of one member but of many. If the foot should say, 'Because I am not a hand, I do not belong to the body,' that would not make it any less a part of the body.

And if the ear should say, 'Because I am not an eye, I do not belong to the body,' that would not make it any less a part of the body.

If the whole body were an eye, where would be the hearing? If the whole body were an ear, where would be the sense of smell? But as it is, God arranged the organs in the body, each one of them, as he chose.

If all were a single organ, where would the body be? As it is, there are many parts, yet one body. The eye cannot say to the hand, 'I have no need of you,' nor again the head to the feet, 'I have no need of you.'

On the contrary, the parts of the body which seem to be weaker are indispensable, and those parts of the body which we think less honorable we invest with the greater honor, and our unpresentable parts are treated with greater modesty, which our more presentable parts do not require.

But God has so adjusted the body, giving the greater honor to the inferior part, that there may be no discord in the body, but that the members may have the same care for one another.

If one member suffers, all suffer together; if one member is honored, all rejoice together."

1 CORINTHIANS 12:14-26

Meditation

While we all should want to ascend to the heights of the spiritual life, we have to remember to "grow where we are planted," as Mother Teresa said. The way in which we live out our devotion to the Lord corresponds to our state in life, as well as our God-given role in the Body of Christ.

And don't think that the daily activities in which we're involved aren't opportunities for growth in sanctity.

As we progress through the spiritual life, we'll come to deeply realize that every person, issue, challenge - every single situation in life - is a golden opportunity for sanctification.

Ask the Lord for help so as to recognize these opportunities, as well as the grace to approach each of them with the love of Christ.

Review Questions

1. What does it mean that our devotion to God is supposed to correspond to our "station in life"?

Discussion Questions

1. How did the story of Mother Theresa's advice to "grow where you are planted" strike you? How might it apply to your own life?

2. Have you ever made the same mistake as Matthew of putting devotion in front of your necessary duties? Give an example.

Prayer Journal

LESSON THREE

How Deification Happens

What We Covered in Our Last Lesson

Everyone, man and woman, prince and pauper, priest and layman - *everyone* is called to live the devout life. However, the way each of us practices devotion is going to differ depending upon our situation. Every one of us has a particular role within society which somewhat dictates the way we practice devotion and grow in the spiritual life. The president or prime minister of a country shouldn't attempt to separate himself like the hermit in a cave. The father of a family can't decide to never save any money like a Capuchin monk. If a mother spent every moment praying in church like a nun, what would become of her family?

Too many times we fall into the trap of thinking that deep spirituality can only be achieved by radically changing everything. That needs to happen *interiorly*, but not necessarily exteriorly. God put us where we are for a reason. He's got a plan, and we've got to grow where he plants us.

Lesson Introduction

In Matthew 5:48, Christ sets a seemingly impossible goal for his followers: "Be perfect, even as your heavenly Father is perfect." Pretty lofty, right?

The question is, "If perfection is the goal, how exactly does it happen?"

Notes

What The Saints Say

"He who was the Son of God became the Son of man, that man ... might become the son of God."

ST. IRENAEUS OF LYONS – *2nd Century Greek Bishop & Author of the classic "Against Heresies"*

Lectio Divina

"I have been crucified with Christ; it is no longer I who live, but Christ who lives in me; and the life I now live in the flesh I live by faith in the Son of God, who loved me and gave himself for me."

GALATIANS 2:20

Meditation

Divinization is nothing less than becoming more like Jesus Christ. And the way this happens is by drawing ever closer to him through the sacraments and a deep life of prayer.

We literally become unified with him. It is a process that begins at baptism, and continues—Lord willing—until the end of our lives.

Really, it's a process of allowing more and more room for the Holy Spirit to operate in our heart. Never forget that He is not a "thing," but a Person - the Third Person of the Most Holy Trinity.

Begin to talk to the Holy Spirit and ask Him to guide you more deeply into the depths of God. His greatest desire is to help you enter into greater union with the Lord.

Review Questions

1. What is the primary way by which we are deified?

2. Which member of the Trinity is particularly at work in our deification?

3. What has to happen for us to become part of the family of God?

4. Do we lose our identity as we become more and more like God?

Discussion Questions

1. Had you ever considered what it means to be a part of the family of God in a real way?

2. How does the fact that you are made for literal divine life in the family of God make you view your life on earth? Does it change your priorities?

Prayer Journal

LESSON FOUR

The Desire for Divinity

What We Covered in Our Last Lesson

By what means do we actually become perfect? The primary answer is grace. It is grace, particularly sanctifying grace, that penetrates into our very soul and perfects us. Little by little, the nourishment received from a life of the sacraments, prayer, and some study, helps us grow in the life of grace. And it all happens through the power of the Holy Spirit. It is the particular task or role of the Holy Spirit to sanctify us and move us down the road to divine life.

We were made for the divine family of God and we can't really, truly be part of that family unless we're really, truly divine like the rest of the family. This is the whole point of the Incarnation, Passion, death and resurrection of Jesus Christ. He became like us so we could become like him.

Through the Paschal Mystery, we are joined to his Mystical Body in such a manner that we pass through his sacred human nature and on into his divine nature. As St. Peter declared, we become "partakers of the divine nature" of God (2 Pt 1:4). However, this does not mean that we lose our personhood or identity. In fact, united to God, we gain a deeper and more incredible identity. We find the fullness of our humanity when we are joined to Jesus Christ through the work of the Holy Spirit.

Even though God offers us this amazing gift of his very divinity, we often reject it because we don't like the responsibility and demands it puts upon us. And yet, God our Father is so patient with us. He is desperate to share his life with us. He is desperate to perfect us so that we become true members of his divine family and join him for all eternity.

Lesson Introduction

Even though Adam and Eve were created in the "image" and "likeness" of Almighty God, they were lacking something - divinity. Even so, they wanted it badly.

And so do we...

Notes

What The Saints Say

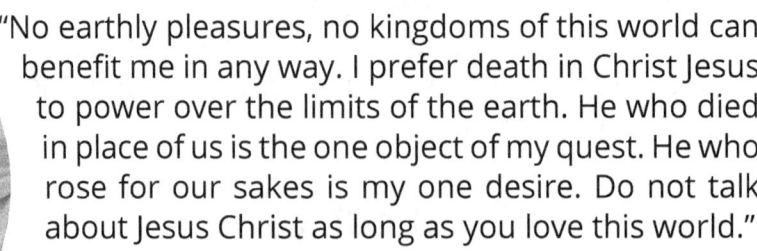

"No earthly pleasures, no kingdoms of this world can benefit me in any way. I prefer death in Christ Jesus to power over the limits of the earth. He who died in place of us is the one object of my quest. He who rose for our sakes is my one desire. Do not talk about Jesus Christ as long as you love this world."

ST. IGNATIUS OF ANTIOCH – *1st Century Bishop of Antioch & Early Christian Martyr*

Lectio Divina

"Then God said, 'Let us make man in our image, after our likeness; and let them have dominion over the fish of the sea, and over the birds of the air, and over the cattle, and over all the earth, and over every creeping thing that creeps upon the earth.'

So God created man in his own image, in the image of God he created him; male and female he created them."

GENESIS 1:26-27

Meditation

The reason each of us has a longing to be divine is because that's what we were created to be from the beginning. That's why Genesis tells us God made Adam and Eve in his "image" and "likeness."

In other words, He made us to be part of his Divine Family.

Divine life is the gnawing in our heart, the hunger that can never be satiated this side of heaven. Unfortunately, we constantly try to satiate this craving with the distractions of this world, though we know they never satisfy.

The "new car smell" always goes away.

But until we realize this, and begin to focus our attention on the only thing that *can* satisfy us - a deep relationship with the God of the universe - we'll never ascend very high on the spiritual ladder.

Ask the Lord in prayer to help you see the shallowness of only living for this world, and to be filled with the desire for Christ alone.

Review Questions

1. Even after being created in the image and likeness of God, what did Adam and Eve still lack?

2. What was wrong with the way that Adam and Eve tried to acquire divinity?

Discussion Questions

1. How does an understanding of the fall of Adam and Eve change your understanding of why Jesus became man? Does it give you a new vision of God's overall plan?

2. Are there areas of your life you are looking to live "on your own terms" instead of God's?

Prayer Journal

LESSON FIVE

The Power of Love to Divinize

What We Covered in Our Last Lesson

The *Catechism of the Catholic Church* declares that "The glory of God is man fully alive," and that we are "created to be his sons" (CCC 294). What an amazing gift God has offered to each and every one of us! But we also know that no one comes out of the box, so to speak, "displaying the glory of God" completely. We are fallen. In fact, even *before* the Fall, there's a sense in which Adam and Eve weren't totally "up to snuff." They lacked a share of God's divine nature which would allow them to fully become part of the family. They weren't fully deified.

What is it that Adam and Eve wanted? What was their temptation all about? They wanted divinity. They wanted to be deified. The serpent's false promise was that if they ate the fruit they would become "like God" (Gen. 3:5).

Wanting to be "like God" was not the problem for Adam and Eve. That's what they were created for. Their problem was that they wanted it on their own terms, not God's. This is our problem, as well.

Our pride constantly declares that we are "number one" and we place ourselves over the top of other people and even God himself. We're following in the footsteps of the *first* Adam, instead of the *New* Adam, Jesus Christ. We have to mature enough to recognize the path to perfection is only through Christ, and follow it constantly. Our deification doesn't only happen later. It's a process that begins on earth, and is completed in heaven.

Lesson Introduction

St. Augustine wrote some beautiful meditations on the vital role of love in the spiritual life. In short, he shows there is nothing more important.

(Much of what is discussed in this lesson is derived from a brilliant book by Fr. Vincent Meconi titled "Called to Be Children of God.")

Notes

What The Saints Say

"Always as a person loves, so he is. Do you love the earth? You will be earth. Do you love God? What shall I say? That you will be God? I don't dare to say this on my own.

Let us listen to the scriptures. ... "You are gods and children of the Most High (Psalm 82:6).""

ST. AUGUSTINE – *4th Century Bishop of Hippo & Doctor of the Church*

Sermon 192.1; Hill, Sermons, vol. III/6 (Hyde Park: N.Y.: New City Press, 1993), 46.

Lectio Divina

"See what love the Father has given us, that we should be called children of God; and so we are. The reason why the world does not know us is that it did not know him.

Beloved, we are God's children now; it does not yet appear what we shall be, but we know that when he appears we shall be like him, for we shall see him as he is.

And every one who thus hopes in him purifies himself as he is pure."

1 JOHN 3:1-3

Meditation

Along with faith and hope, love is one of the three theological virtues. And while they're all important, Scripture is clear that the greatest of these is love. (1 Cor. 13:13)

But why is it that love has the power to divinize?

In short, it's because "God is love," as 1 John 4:8 declares. If we want to be like God, we have to learn to love. And remember that love doesn't necessarily mean feelings. It's an act of the will that involves the whole person. That doesn't mean that feelings won't often be present. They will.

That said, you can love someone without actually liking them. Again, it's primarily an act of the will that desires the best for that person in Christian charity.

So if you're struggling to love, simply pray: "Lord, you know I'm struggling with this situation. Help me to love as you do."

And if your struggle involves a particular person, a sure way to help you grow in love is to repeatedly offer prayers for that person over a period of time. It's not always easy, but it's supremely effective.

Offering prayers for the well-being of a person with whom you're struggling is a great act of the will, and an indicator that you're beginning to love like Christ.

Review Questions

1. According to St. John the Evangelist and St. Augustine, what is the key to the entire process of deification?

2. According to St. Augustine, what is the "great exchange of nature"?

Discussion Questions

1. How does St. Augustine's unpacking of the power of love transform your understanding of this chief of the theological virtues? Does St. Augustine help you to understand why love is the principle of everything?

2. How does a deeper understanding of the gift God is offering (i.e. divinity) affect your love for Him and your desire to grow in the spiritual life?

Prayer Journal

LESSON SIX

The Beauty of Grace

What We Covered in Our Last Lesson

In paragraph 221, the *Catechism of the Catholic Church* says, "God's very being is love. By sending his only Son and the Spirit of Love in the fullness of time, God has revealed his innermost secret: God himself is an eternal exchange of love, Father, Son and Holy Spirit, and he has destined us to share in that exchange."

The transformative power of love is the secret to understanding how deification actually works. It's the key to our partaking of the divine nature of God. Love, says St. Augustine, changes our very identity. We become what we love. In other words, love doesn't just unite, it transforms.

Through humble *love* Our Lord shared himself with us by becoming the bridge between humanity and divinity. "In order to make gods of those who were merely human, one who was God made himself human," says Augustine. As theologians put it, his *kenosis* - his self-emptying - leads to our *theosis* - our deification.

The entire movement of the Christian life is toward transformation. For the love of God and who he is, we need to move toward perfection. When we grow in love of God, we don't just stop doing bad things because we feel differently toward God. We stop because we are literally being transformed into his likeness. God is love. And that love - poured into our hearts - is what transforms us.

Lesson Introduction

It's time to pivot to the topic of grace.

Among other things, we'll get into sanctifying and actual grace, how Adam and Eve lost grace and what it means for us. We're also going to talk about the soul and what it means to be a human person created in the image of God.

In some ways, this is the deepest of all the sections in the Science of Sainthood. Some of what you're going to encounter in these lessons might make you scratch your head at first because we'll go a bit "next level" in some areas. And that should excite you.

Because learning new things is great, especially when it has to do with getting to heaven!

Notes

_____
_____
_____
_____
_____
_____
_____
_____

What The Saints Say

"Nothing whatever pertaining to godliness and real holiness can be accomplished without grace."

ST. AUGUSTINE - *4th Century Bishop of Hippo & Doctor of the Church*

Lectio Divina

"Therefore, since we are justified by faith, we have peace with God through our Lord Jesus Christ. Through him we have obtained access to this grace in which we stand, and we rejoice in our hope of sharing the glory of God.

More than that, we rejoice in our sufferings, knowing that suffering produces endurance, and endurance produces character, and character produces hope, and hope does not disappoint us, because God's love has been poured into our hearts through the Holy Spirit who has been given to us."

ROMANS 5:1-5

Meditation

The grace of God is worth more than we can possibly imagine. It's the key to everything. And realize we're not just talking about eternal life. Grace is the key to our lives on earth, as well.

It is grace that gives us the ability to deal with all that the world throws our way. It is grace that gives us the strength to pick ourselves up after falling into sin, so as to begin anew. It is grace that gives us the power to live and love like God.

Grace is everything.

And yet, how often do we turn our backs on this magnificent help given to us by God? How often do we spurn the greatest gift that could ever be given?

Review Questions

1. Since God literally dwells inside of us, what does St. Paul call our body in 1 Corinthians 6?

2. While all three members of the Trinity dwell inside of us when we're in a state of grace, which member is particularly mentioned by St. Paul? Why?

Discussion Questions

1. Did you ever consider that through grace our union with the God of the universe is similar to that which exists between the Son and the Father through the Holy Spirit? How does that make you feel?

2. How does the fact that God makes his home inside of you make you feel about sin in your life? About growth in virtue?

Prayer Journal

LESSON SEVEN

Why Do We Struggle?
Unpacking the "Absolute Supernatural"

What We Covered in Our Last Lesson

There is a reality to the literal indwelling of the Trinity in our lives through grace. As St. Paul asks in 1 Corinthians 6:19, "Do you not know that your body is a temple of the Holy Spirit within you, which you have from God?" So God dwells in *us* before we dwell with *him* in heaven. He makes his kingdom within us. And it's in this interior kingdom that we grow in the mystical life. The more we make ourselves his sons and daughters through growth in virtue and holiness, the deeper our familial union with the king.

Because of the amazing power of grace, our union with the God of the universe is similar to that which exists between the Son and the Father through the Holy Spirit. This is exactly what Christ prays for in the famous High Priestly prayer in John chapter 17 when he says, "...for those who believe in me through their word, that they may all be one; even as thou, Father, art in me, and I in thee" (17:20-21). It's a prayer for us to be elevated into divinity, to become "like God"!

In fact, St. Thomas Aquinas says people progressing on the road to divinity actually enjoy the divine Person himself. And this union gets so intense that words fail even the most eloquent mystic at the higher levels of the spiritual life. True union with himself is the goal of everything God has given to us, and it all revolves around grace.

Lesson Introduction

If we're going to understand what grace is, what it does, and what deification is all about (i.e. the entire goal and direction of the Christian life), we have to really understand how we're made and what went wrong.

In other words, we need to answer the question, "Why do we struggle?" What really happened back in the Garden of Eden that made this whole path more than a little difficult?

This session is a little more "next level" than most, but it's important that we discuss this, so as to truly understand how amazing God's gift of grace to us is.

▶ PLAY VIDEO

Notes

What The Saints Say

"We are then burdened with this corruptible body; but knowing that the cause of this burdensomeness is not the nature and substance of the body, but its corruption, we do not desire to be deprived of the body, but to be clothed with its immortality.

For then, also, there will be a body, but it shall no longer be a burden, being no longer corruptible."

ST. AUGUSTINE - *4th Century Bishop of Hippo & Doctor of the Church*

Lectio Divina

"But I say, walk by the Spirit, and do not gratify the desires of the flesh. For the desires of the flesh are against the Spirit, and the desires of the Spirit are against the flesh; for these are opposed to each other, to prevent you from doing what you would.

But if you are led by the Spirit you are not under the law.

Now the works of the flesh are plain: immorality, impurity, licentiousness, idolatry, sorcery, enmity, strife, jealousy, anger, selfishness, dissension, party spirit, envy, drunkenness, carousing, and the like. I warn you, as I warned you before, that those who do such things shall not inherit the kingdom of God.

But the fruit of the Spirit is love, joy, peace, patience, kindness, goodness, faithfulness, gentleness, self-control; against such there is no law.

And those who belong to Christ Jesus have crucified the flesh with its passions and desires."

GALATIANS 5:16-24

Meditation

At some point in the spiritual life, you come to the place where you begin to take a hard look at your life. You begin to examine all the different areas in your life and weigh their value on the scale of eternity. This is a huge moment in your move toward God. It's a sign of progress.

And it's something that needs to happen on a regular basis. Why? Because the world is constantly appealing to our "flesh," our lower nature. Fueled by the twisted desire of the Evil One, the world tempts us with every sin imaginable.

For this reason, we must "crucify the flesh" as St. Paul says. We must calm our passions and desires, and seek what is above. This is what sets us apart and marks us as children of Almighty God.

Review Questions

1. If we want to live a moral life, what three things need to be in control of our actions?

2. While pleasure is good in and of itself, when does it become wrong?

3. What does St. Paul mean when he talks about a battle between our flesh and spirit in the book of Galatians?

Discussion Questions

1. What were some of the ideas you heard for the first time in this lesson?

2. How did this lesson give you a new and deeper understanding of sanctifying grace?

Prayer Journal

LESSON EIGHT

Why Do We Struggle?

Understanding the "Relative Supernatural"

What We Covered in Our Last Lesson

Created in the image of God, we are a union of body and soul. We are a contact point between the spiritual and natural worlds, between heaven and earth. In the beginning, Adam wasn't deified, but he was in harmony with God. His higher faculties, his reason (intellect) and will, ruled over his lower faculties and passions.

But because of the Fall, our lower faculties - the vegetative and animal senses and passions, are more in control than they should be. They rebel against our higher, more "angelic" faculties - our reason (intellect) and will. However, just because we're now disordered doesn't mean we've lost the war. There's always the power to resist.

According to spiritual theologian, Fr. Adolphe Tanquerey, there are two different kinds, or levels, of supernatural gifts. They are called the "absolute" supernatural and the "relative" supernatural. "Absolute" supernatural is when someone or something is supernatural in its very essence. The "absolute" supernatural totally transcends nature and can't be merited by a creature. We can't earn it and we have no rights to it. There are only two instances of the "absolute" supernatural: the Incarnation of Jesus Christ and sanctifying grace.

In the Incarnation, Christ united humanity with his divinity in such a way that while they are inseparably blended and yet mysteriously remain distinct - a human nature and a divine nature - they form the one person of Jesus Christ. This is the highest instance of the "absolute" supernatural.

The second instance of the "absolute supernatural" is sanctifying grace, which we receive through the sacraments. It's "absolutely" supernatural, but to a lesser degree than the Incarnation. Sanctifying grace doesn't make us God, but it makes us *like* God, which is the goal of the spiritual life. The Catechism says, "the grace of Christ is the gratuitous gift that God makes to us of his own life" (CCC 1999).

Lesson Introduction

Most of us have little idea of the real meaning and power of the sacraments. We don't know why they're so essential. And that's because we've probably never dug very deeply into their backstory.

What God did in the beginning for Adam and Eve is the first scene of the movie of our life. And understanding it helps us not only make sense of all those things we had to memorize (or never knew) as kids, but also why they are such powerful weapons in our lifelong struggle toward holiness.

So in this lesson we're going to investigate what Adam had and lost, which will give us much more appreciation for what we now have through Christ. It will also help illuminate the spiritual life in general.

Notes

What The Saints Say

"Man was made after the image and likeness of God; but sin marred the beauty of the image by dragging the soul down to passionate desires.

Now, God, who made man, is the true life. Therefore, when man lost his likeness to God, he lost his participation in the true life; separated and estranged from God as he is, it is impossible for him to enjoy the blessedness of the divine life.

Let us return, then, to the grace [which was ours] in the beginning and from which we have alienated ourselves by sin, and let us again adorn ourselves with the beauty of God's image, being made like to our Creator through the quieting of our passions."

ST. BASIL THE GREAT – *4th Century Bishop of Caesarea & Doctor of the Church*

Lectio Divina

"I do not understand my own actions. For I do not do what I want, but I do the very thing I hate."

ROMANS 7:15

Meditation

St. Paul nails it. The spiritual life is a struggle. It's a war. And oftentimes we find ourselves doing the very things we want to avoid.

How often have we described the same weakness to our priest? How often do we find ourselves confessing the same sins over and over?

But while sin is never "okay," the fact that we continue to get up and push forward is a great indicator of spiritual growth.

Don't ever lose hope. We are children of God...for real. And as long as we remain faithful, the Lord will help us crush our sins and conform ourselves to his beautiful heart.

Review Questions

1. What were Adam's three preternatural gifts?

2. For what special gift were the preternatural gifts preparing Adam?

3. What other beings besides Adam have infused knowledge?

Discussion Questions

1. Why should we not simply blame our sinful actions on Adam?

2. Are there particular areas in your life where you have basically given up trying to get better? What might be the solution?

Prayer Journal

LESSON NINE

Sanctifying Grace & Our Formal Participation in God

What We Covered in Our Last Lesson

Adam possessed gifts that theologians call the "relative" supernatural. This means that the gifts he received from God gave Adam abilities that would normally be *beyond* his natural abilities, but not supernatural in their essence. They were only supernatural to him as a human. Many theologians hold that Adam received three relative supernatural, or preternatural gifts: infused knowledge, control of the passions, and immortality of the body.

God gave Adam infused knowledge because he was supposed to be the first educator of all of humanity. With this gift, Adam's knowledge far exceeded ours. Also, it was easy for him to control his passions. The possibility of sin still existed, but Adam didn't have the overwhelming urges and struggles that we often have to fight. Finally, Adam had immortality of body, meaning that had he not sinned, he would have lived forever. These "preternatural" gifts were preparation for sanctifying grace.

Even though Adam's fall from grace affected us, we can't use him as an excuse for our personal sin. The grace God gives is far more powerful than the negative effect of Adam's fall. As St. Paul said in Romans 5:20, "Where sin increased, grace abounded all the more."

Lesson Introduction

The question we now have to ask ourselves is, "What were Adam's three preternatural gifts preparing him for?" Because remember, as amazing as they were, the gifts of infused knowledge, control of the passions, and immortality of the body were not the end game.

The real gift, the real prize, has always been sanctifying grace. Why? Because only it has the power to give us something beyond our wildest dreams…divinity.

Notes

What The Saints Say

"All these things then Paul calls a 'superabundance' of grace (Rom. 5:17), showing that what we received was not a medicine only to counterbalance the wound, but even health, and comeliness, and honor, and glory and dignities far transcending our natural state."

ST. JOHN CHRYSOSTOM – *4th Century Archbishop of Constantinople & Doctor of the Church*

Willis, J. R. (Ed.). (2002). The Teachings of the Church Fathers (p. 241). San Francisco: Ignatius Press.

Lectio Divina

"And the Word became flesh and dwelt among us, full of grace and truth; we have beheld his glory, glory as of the only Son from the Father.

(John bore witness to him, and cried, 'This was he of whom I said, "He who comes after me ranks before me, for he was before me."') And from his fulness have we all received, grace upon grace."

JOHN 1:14-16

Meditation

Think about this: the Second Person of the Most Holy Trinity literally "dwelt among us" lowly humans. More literally in Greek, he "pitched his tent" or "tabernacled" among us.

As scholar Curtis Mitch points out in the Ignatius Catholic Study Bible, "John is making a link between the Incarnation of Jesus and the erection of the wilderness Tabernacle in the Old Testament (Ex 25:8–9)."

The Tabernacle was the actual dwelling place of God in the Old Testament. It was the place of sacrifice and worship for the Israelites as they wandered in the wilderness.

But as incredible as it was that Almighty God dwelt among his people in that manner, the opportunity before each of us is far more amazing. St. John declares that Christ gives us "grace upon grace."

In other words, the graces of the Old Covenant have been superseded by the transformative grace of Jesus Christ. And unlike in Old Testament days, he doesn't live in some separate building. He literally dwells inside of us!

Review Questions

1. Is it correct to say that sanctifying grace is a substance? Explain your answer.

2. In what does sanctifying grace allow us to participate?

Discussion Questions

1. Does the fact that you literally and formally participate in the life of God through grace affect your desire for the sacraments?

2. How does the gift of grace deepen your understanding of the Fatherhood of God?

Prayer Journal

LESSON TEN

The "Accident" of Sanctifying Grace

What We Covered in Our Last Lesson

Sanctifying grace is what transforms us into children of God. Infused at baptism, it incorporates us into the Mystical Body of Christ. Sometimes called "habitual grace," sanctifying grace is the key to the spiritual life in many ways.

Grace is supernatural, which means it isn't a substance. Nevertheless, sanctifying grace is real. It seeps into the very marrow of our soul, penetrating to our very essence. It manifests itself through the virtues, transforming our soul and making it pleasing to God. In fact, it makes us so pleasing to God that the soul becomes God's dwelling place, his Temple.

Sanctifying grace is so powerful that it makes us, fallen as we are, beautiful beyond compare. Through it we really, formally participate in the divine life of our Father. God really becomes Our Father. Jesus truly becomes our brother. It is a "formal" participation in the divine life of God, not simply "virtual" (i.e. shared in a way different from the source). Put simply, sanctifying grace is so potent that once we have it, there is no difference between the life of God in which we share, and God himself.

Lesson Introduction

While we participate in a totally real way in the divinity of Our Lord, that participation is what we call "accidental."

That doesn't mean it only happened by accident. It means that our participation in the divine nature is just that, a participation. And this is a huge point to ponder so that we understand what is happening as we ascend the divine ladder to God.

Notes

What The Saints Say

"Adam sinned and earned all sorrows;—likewise the world after his example, all guilt.—And instead of considering how it should be restored,—considered how its fall should be pleasant for it.

Glory to Him Who came and restored it! This cause summoned Him that is pure,—that He should come and he baptized, even He with the defiled,— Heaven for His glory was rent asunder.

That the purifier of all might be baptized with all,—He came down and sanctified the water for our baptism."

ST. EPHREM THE SYRIAN – *4th Century Theologian & Deacon*
Willis, J. R. (Ed.). (2002). The Teachings of the Church Fathers (p. 239). San Francisco: Ignatius Press.

Lectio Divina

"Law came in, to increase the trespass; but where sin increased, grace abounded all the more, so that, as sin reigned in death, grace also might reign through righteousness to eternal life through Jesus Christ our Lord."

ROMANS 5:20-21

Meditation

In the Old Testament, the law was given to show the Israelites what was right and wrong. But what it didn't provide them was the ability to actually do the right thing.

Like the Israelites, we basically know what we're supposed to do. But thanks be to God that he not only tells us what to do, he gives us the power to obey.

That's the beauty of grace. The question is, "Are we going to use it?"

Review Questions

1. Is the goal of Catholic spirituality to lose our personal identity in God? Explain your answer.

2. When we are in a state of grace, does the Holy Spirit dwell in our body, our spirit, or both?

3. What's another name for the *ruach*, or breath of God, that He breathed into Adam's nostrils in the Garden of Eden?

Discussion Questions

1. Does a deeper understanding of the value of sanctifying grace make you rethink the seriousness of mortal sin?

2. What are some practical ways you can become more open to God's grace?

Prayer Journal

LESSON ELEVEN

Understanding the Two Regions of the Human Soul

What We Covered in Our Last Lesson

While we truly participate in the divinity of Our Lord, that participation is what we call "accidental." In other words, our participation in the divine nature is just that, a *participation*. We don't become God. We "participate" in him. He divinizes us in a way that doesn't change who we are.

Since we're creatures, when sanctifying grace is given to us, it is finite - it's limited. Grace *elevates* our nature, but doesn't change it. That's why receiving sanctifying grace doesn't turn us into God. The Fathers of the Church say that when in a state of grace, we become living images of the Blessed Trinity. It's as if the Holy Spirit impresses his features upon us like a seal impresses an image on hot wax. This is what gives us immeasurable beauty in God's eyes. So sanctifying grace gives us *something* of God's life, but not his essence.

Through grace, we literally receive the most Holy Trinity into the depths of our soul. In fact, the indwelling of the Three Persons of the Trinity is total – both physical and moral. The Holy Spirit dwells in the whole person, body and soul.

And since God now dwells so intimately inside of us, a sweet familiarity exists that wasn't present before we possessed this grace. Through sanctifying grace, we can communicate more intimately with him. In fact, he doesn't just communicate with us. He communicates himself *to* us, and he is even closer to us than we are to ourselves.

Lesson Introduction

Truly understanding the human soul before we move further into the Science of Sainthood is absolutely necessary. Why? Because it helps us to understand who we are as human persons, and what we're made to be.

That said, this is a lesson on which you might need to spend a bit more time. Some of the material might be new. But when you begin to see how it all fits together, you'll more deeply understand why you do the things you do...and the incredible power of God's grace!

Notes

What The Saints Say

"And inasmuch as there are three things of which man consists,—namely, spirit, soul, and body—which again are spoken of as two, because frequently the soul is named along with the spirit; for a certain rational position of the same, of which beasts are devoid, is called spirit: the principal part in us is the spirit."

ST. AUGUSTINE - *4th Century Bishop of Hippo & Doctor of the Church*

Willis, J. R. (Ed.). (2002). The Teachings of the Church Fathers (p. 222). San Francisco: Ignatius Press.

Lectio Divina

"And do not fear those who kill the body but cannot kill the soul; rather fear him who can destroy both soul and body in hell."

MATTHEW 10:28

Meditation

Don't be afraid of men who can only take your earthly life. Be afraid of the Evil One who wants to destroy your soul.

Christ is pretty clear.

But there's another, more spiritual level according to the Ignatius Catholic Study Bible: "Jesus uses this distinction between body and soul to contrast the relative value of earthly life with the absolute good of eternal life in heaven."[1]

In other words, why do we constantly turn our backs on the offer of a lifetime in heaven for the lesser, "limited time only" offer of this world?

We shouldn't just fear the fires of hell. We should fear the loss of the undreamed-of ecstatic union with the God of the Universe.

That's the union for which we were made. And that union can only happen by utilizing the power of grace to put our spiritual house in order.

"Lord, help me calm my passions, lift my eyes to heaven, and abandon myself to you!"

The Ignatius Catholic Study Bible: The New Testament *(p. 24). San Francisco: Ignatius Press.*

Review Questions

1. What are the formal names for the two parts of the soul?

2. What are the things that live in the "downstairs" part of the soul? What lives upstairs?

3. While ours remains superior, with what do we share the traits of the "downstairs" of our soul? With whom do we share the traits of the "upstairs" of our soul?

Discussion Questions

1. Does understanding the division of the soul help you understand why you do certain things and act in certain ways? How?

2. Are there areas in your life that are dominated by the "downstairs" of your soul?

Prayer Journal

LESSON TWELVE

The Fall from Grace

What We Covered in Our Last Lesson

In its "natural" state, the human soul is divided into two regions, kind of like an "upstairs" and "downstairs" of a house. The downstairs, so to speak, is what we call the "sensible" order. The upstairs is called the "supra-sensible," or "intellectual" order.

In the sensible order (downstairs) reside your external senses - what you can see, taste, touch, smell, and hear. But there's more living down there, too. Namely, what we can call "internal" senses. These consist of your imagination, your sensible memory, as well as passions and emotions. The sensible order is common to both men and animals. However, they're not equal. Since humans are made in the image of God, our sensible order is of a higher order than the animals.

Then there's the upstairs, what we call the supra-sensible, or intellectual, part of the soul. This is the residence of the intellect and will (and memory). Why is it higher than the sensible order? Because instead of sharing these traits of the soul with animals, we share them with angels (though theirs is of a higher order). It's because of this "intellectual" part of the soul that we call the soul "spiritual."

Lesson Introduction

Why did Jesus come and do what he did? Why did he become like us and institute a sacramental system of grace? As usual, when it comes to God, it goes back to the beginning. It all goes back to Adam and the garden of Eden, which we've already discussed a bit.

But now we're going to finish off the story of how Adam "finished" us off. Well, maybe he didn't finish us off, but he certainly made things a bit more difficult. He's the one who made the spiritual life a bit of an uphill climb.

Notes

What The Saints Say

"Sin is a turning away from God and a turning towards creatures. After the angels were created by the goodness of God out of nothing they were subjected to a moral testing.

The good angels who passed the test were rewarded with the beatific vision; the bad angels were rejected and through their own fault merited consignment to hell.

Our first parents underwent a similar testing, but sinned seriously and lost both the preternatural gifts of great knowledge, self-control, freedom from suffering and death, and the supernatural gifts of sanctifying grace and the infused virtues of faith, hope, and charity.

As a result, every person born into this world is born with original sin, the deprivation of grace caused by the free act of sin committed by the head of the race, for original sin is transmitted by natural generation.

Those who die in the state of original sin are excluded from the beatific vision of God."

ST. AUGUSTINE - *4th Century Bishop of Hippo & Doctor of the Church*
Willis, J. R. (Ed.). (2002). The Teachings of the Church Fathers (p. 233). San Francisco: Ignatius Press.

Lectio Divina

"Yet death reigned from Adam to Moses, even over those whose sins were not like the transgression of Adam, who was a type of the one who was to come. But the free gift is not like the trespass.

For if many died through one man's trespass, much more have the grace of God and the free gift in the grace of that one man Jesus Christ abounded for many."

ROMANS 5:14-15

Meditation

The Original Sin of Adam crushed us. It wrecked our union with God.

And perhaps there are times when we feel this state of affairs is a bit unfair; like somehow we got the short end of the stick. After all, we didn't sin in the Garden of Eden. Some other guy committed the crime, so why do we have to suffer the consequences? We could have all been hanging out in an earthly paradise!

But we must remember that we're all connected. Adam represented all of us theologically. And yes, when he went down, we all went down. But don't forget that there's also a silver lining. Since we're all part of the same human family represented by Christ, when He opened the path to divinity, He opened it for everyone.

And the gift of divine life offered by Christ far exceeds both the earthly paradise and incredible spiritual gifts given to Adam. Don't ever undervalue what God has given us.

"Thank you, Lord, for giving me a share of your divinity. And may I always immediately return to your loving embrace when I sin and forsake your incredible gift."

Review Questions

1. Did Adam understand the consequences of his disobedience to God's command not to eat the fruit of the tree of knowledge of good and evil?

2. What major sin was the root of Adam's fall?

3. What did Adam and Eve lose when they sinned?

Discussion Questions

1. Does the fact that Adam still fell even with all the preternatural gifts from God make you a little more aware of the powerful deceit wielded by the Evil One?

2. How does understanding the humble love of Christ affect your view of Adam's failure in the Garden?

Prayer Journal

LESSON THIRTEEN

Introduction to Actual Grace & Free Will

What We Covered in Our Last Lesson

In spite of all the very powerful preternatural gifts that Adam possessed, he was still free. He could make choices. And when put to the test by God, Adam's responsibility was to use all the amazing gifts God gave him in accordance with God's command.

From a rational human standpoint, Adam was probably looking at the fruit of the tree of the knowledge of good and evil thinking "I wonder why I can't have it." After all, he was Adam. He had dominion over creation. And yet God told Adam "don't eat the fruit."

The point is that God's command supersedes the human understanding of what is and isn't good. But through pride, Adam chose human reason over divine reason. He decided God didn't know best and chose to disobey even though he knew what would happen if he rebelled.

By rights, God could have taken Adam and Eve out right when they sinned. But instead of a crazy, power-hungry maniac, he's a merciful *Father*. So like a good parent, he took away his children's privileges. He stripped Adam and Eve of the gifts of integrity and sanctifying grace. But that's not all he did.

As a loving Father, he gave them faith and hope, which was a kind of divine condescension after their fall from grace. To save them from that spiral of anguish and desperation, God gave them hope in a Redeemer who would straighten things out and faith that what was done could one day be undone.

Lesson Introduction

God not only offers us salvation through his grace, he even gives grace to help us *receive* grace. It's like taking a test where our hands are actually guided to mark the appropriate box while the answers are being whispered in our ear.

And even though he constantly bombards us with these "actual graces," God gives us the freedom and power to refuse them. The question is, "Why?"

Notes

What The Saints Say

"All depends indeed on God, but not so that our free-will is hindered. 'If then it depend on God, [one says], "why does He blame us?"'

On this account I said, 'so that our free-will is not hindered.' It depends then on us, and on Him. For we must first choose the good; and then He leads us to His own.

He does not anticipate our choice, lest our free-will should be outraged. But when we have chosen, then great is the assistance He brings to us...."

ST. JOHN CHRYSOSTOM - *4th Century Archbishop of Constantinople & Doctor of the Church*

Willis, J. R. (Ed.). (2002). The Teachings of the Church Fathers (p. 251). San Francisco: Ignatius Press.

Lectio Divina

"'My grace is sufficient for you, for my power is made perfect in weakness.' I will all the more gladly boast of my weaknesses, that the power of Christ may rest upon me.

For the sake of Christ, then, I am content with weaknesses, insults, hardships, persecutions, and calamities; for when I am weak, then I am strong."

2 CORINTHIANS 12:9-10

Meditation

Why did the Lord declare to St. Paul that his "power is made perfect in weakness"? What is the spiritual logic at play? Well, ask yourself this: when does St. Paul say we are most powerful?

Is it when we finally stop gossiping about other people? Is it when we finally stop wasting so much time on the web? Is it when we finally grow enough spiritually that we can finally endure the announcements at the end of a long Mass? The answer is "no" on all three counts.

The Lord says our power has nothing to do with spiritual "victories," so to speak.

We are most strong when we are weak. Why? Because when we finally recognize our weakness and give it over to the Lord, he fills up the space we cleared for him. We're no longer struggling forward on our own power.

The Lord himself fills up the gap in our weakness and ignites our spiritual booster rockets. That's why the weaker we are, the more powerful we become. The supernatural strength we begin to wield is that of Christ.

"Oh Lord, please help me to grow in humility. Help me recognize my weakness, give it to you, and allow you to take control of my life."

Review Questions

1. How would you define actual grace? Sanctifying grace?

2. Is actual grace permanent?

Discussion Questions

1. Have you ever considered how patient God is with you? How does this knowledge make you feel toward Him?

2. What does God's incredible patience with our personal weaknesses teach us about how we should deal with others?

3. Can you think of times in your life when you have deliberately refused the actual graces God was giving you? What happened as a result?

Prayer Journal

LESSON FOURTEEN

Operating Grace vs Cooperating Grace

What We Covered in Our Last Lesson

Once Adam fell, he no longer represented all of humanity and lost the ability to pass on the sanctifying grace he had been originally given. The only way sanctifying grace could be reinstated to everyone would be through a new representative, a "New" Adam, which was exactly God's plan.

Through Christ, not only did we get back what Adam lost, we got more. We got an opportunity to be part of the family of God in a way Adam was not. And one of the major forces God uses to help us move back into the family is something called "actual grace."

Actual grace is the constant nudge God gives us so that we'll move toward him, so we'll turn and receive sanctifying grace. Unlike sanctifying grace, actual grace is not permanent. It's temporary. Its job is to prompt us in the moment to perform some work in relation to justification, sanctification, or salvation. Actual graces are the little "holy helps" that lead us to perfection and help prevent the loss of sanctifying grace. In other words, God not only offers us salvation through his grace, he even *gives* grace to help us *receive* grace.

That said, we have the power to resist actual graces. But God patiently waits for us (and provides more grace) until we finally realize our job is not resistance, but cooperation with the actual graces he provides.

Of course, even our cooperation is a gift of grace. St. Augustine said that "In the business of salvation all is the gift of God." There is nothing in the process of getting to heaven that is exclusively ours. Created in his image, God gives us freedom. But even our free will is a gift from God. He is the cause of our freedom. It is a gift from God, and because he loves us, he provides actual grace to help us make the right choices with this gift of freedom.

Lesson Introduction

While the major distinctions in the life of grace are between sanctifying and actual grace, we can break down actual grace a little further. It can be divided into what we call "operating grace" and "cooperating grace."

What's the difference and why does it matter? That's our topic in this session of the Science of Sainthood.

Notes

What The Saints Say

"On the contrary, Augustine says 'God by co-operating with us, perfects what He began by operating in us, since He who perfects by co-operation with such as are willing, begins by operating that they may will.'

But the operations of God whereby He moves us to good pertain to grace. Therefore grace is fittingly divided into operating and co-operating."

ST. THOMAS AQUINAS – *13th Century Dominican Theologian & Doctor of the Church*

Thomas Aquinas. (n.d.). Summa theologica. (Fathers of the English Dominican Province, Trans.). London: Burns Oates & Washbourne.

Lectio Divina

"But by the grace of God I am what I am, and his grace toward me was not in vain.

On the contrary, I worked harder than any of them, though it was not I, but the grace of God which is with me."

1 CORINTHIANS 15:10

Meditation

While we must constantly strive to grow in the spiritual life, we have to always remember that every single thing we do is the result of grace.

You can't even blink an eye or lift a finger without grace.

As the Catechism of the Catholic Church says, "Grace is favor, the free and undeserved help that God gives us to respond to his call to become children of God, adoptive sons, partakers of the divine nature and of eternal life" (n. 1996).

As you become more attuned to the life of grace, you become more sensitive to the movement of the Holy Spirit. You'll also begin to more deeply understand that the more we give in to the Spirit in our quest for holiness, the faster our progress will be.

As St. Augustine exclaimed, "O Holy Spirit, descend plentifully into my heart. Enlighten the dark corners of this neglected dwelling and scatter there Thy cheerful beams."

Review Questions

1. How would you define cooperating grace? Operating grace?

2. What is our primary responsibility when it comes to grace?

3. What is the number one method to make sure you're not wasting grace?

Discussion Questions

1. Discuss a situation when you experienced a special, operating grace from God.

1. How has this study of grace impacted your view of God's desire for your salvation?

Prayer Journal

Summary Of Lesson 14

According to Fr. Garrigou-Lagrange, the movement of actual grace happens in two different ways. The first way is that it proposes some object which attracts it (like a scripture verse that jumps out at us while reading). The second is when the movement happens from an interior impulse or illumination that can only come from God (like when you suddenly feel moved or inspired to pray).

Actual grace can also be divided into "cooperating grace" and "operating grace." Cooperating grace works along with your actions according to your normal human pattern. For example, it's grace that moves when you pray your daily rosary. On the other hand, operating grace is more of a sudden inspiration from God that is not according to your normal pattern. For example, you're standing in the grocery store and feel a sudden urge to pray.

Regardless of which type of grace we're encountering, our job is to let it flow and to act on it. Whether it's the more yeoman-like action required by cooperating grace, or the more passive mode of operating grace, we have to respond. We have to act. Otherwise, the grace is wasted.

Regular prayer is the key to not wasting grace. It tunes us into God's frequency so that we recognize when grace is being given and increases our ability to receive it.

Take the next step!

Go to ScienceOfSainthood.com today and experience a whole new level of prayer and relationship with God!

"Blown away"

"I can hardly believe how wonderful this is."

Courses in the Science of Sainthood include:

Introduction to Real Prayer

The 7 Deadly Sins

The Moral Virtues

The Theological Virtues

The Dark Night of the Soul

Total Abandonment to God's Will

St. Teresa of Avila's 9 Grades of Prayer

The Gifts of the Spirt ...and more!

"If you've ever wanted to deepen your life of prayer and actually make some progress in avoiding vice and growing in virtue, then look no further. The Science of Sainthood is for you."

–**Dr. Brant Pitre**, Renowned theologian & author of Jesus and the Jewish Roots of the Eucharist

ScienceofSainthood.com

Scan the QR Code with your Phone's Camera & Tap the Link!

"A theological thrill ride!"
–**Mark Hart**, *Executive Vice-President of LifeTeen International*

"I guarantee you will walk away from this book with an intense desire to live in deeper communion with the Lord."
–**Curtis Mitch**, *Author & Editor of the* Ignatius Catholic Study Bible

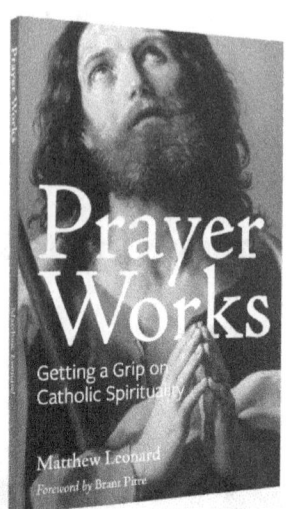

Want more spiritual nourishment?

Check out **The Art of Catholic podcast**. Available on Youtube, iTunes, Spotify, Amazon, and more!

Podcast Heaven ★★★★★
by Trevor-Fooling

Awesome. ★★★★★
by Harleypierrepont

Truth BOMB ★★★★★
by BC Raven 44

Out. Of. The. Park. ★★★★★
by Bobby McQuin

www.ingramcontent.com/pod-product-compliance
Lightning Source LLC
Chambersburg PA
CBHW060426010526
44118CB00017B/2384